Splitting the Atom
& Other Yo-Yo Stuff

by Richie

published by Butterfingers

The Blurb

Splitting the Atom & other Yo-Yo stuff
by Richie
Copyright © R.D.Windsor 1997
All rights reserved.

First edition
Published by Butterfingers, Bristol.

The right of R. D. "Richie" Windsor to be identified as the author of this work has been asserted in accordance with sections 77 and 78 of the Copyright, Designs and Patents Act 1988.

No part of this publication may be stored in a retrieval system, transmitted, or reproduced in any way, including but not by way of limitation, photocopy, photograph, magnetic or other record without the prior written agreement of the publisher.

ISBN 1-898591-16-4

Illustrations by "Mark"
Layout & Design by Charlie Dancey.
Printed by Devenish & Co. Bath.

Splitting the Atom

INTRODUCTION

Welcome to the essential guide for anyone who owns a yo-yo.

Within these pages you'll find hints, tips and tricks of all kinds from an acclaimed master of the yo-yo that will take you from your first faltering yo's to the staggeringly skillsome "Splitting the Atom".

Have fun!

CONTENTS

How your Yo-Yo works 4
Getting started 5
The Sleeper 6
The Slapper 6
Hop the Fence 7
Walk the Dog 8
Two Dogs 8
The Creeper 9
Jump the Dog 10
Spaghetti 11
The Forward Pass 12
Around the World 13
Breakaway 14
The Drawback 15
The 3rd Dimension 16
Monkey Climbs the String 17
Elevator 17
Rock the Baby 18
Out with the Bathwater 18
Pinwheels 19
Sidewinder 19
Flying Saucer 20
Loop the Loop 21
3 Leaf Clover 22

Splitting the Atom

CONTENTS

- Shoot for the Moon 23
- Warp Drive 24
- Dragster 25
- Sky Rocket 26
- Skin the Cat 27
- Orbit Launch 28
- Guillotine 28
- Kick Over 28
- Rock the Baby on the Launchpad .29
- Pullovers 30
- Shooting Star 31
- Rock the Baby under the Stars . .31
- Trapeze 32
- Rock the Baby on the Trapeze . . .33
- Double or Nothing 34
- Double Skin the Cat 35
- Stop and Go 36
- Brain Twister 37
- Finger Hop a.k.a. Roller Coaster .38
- Barrel Rolls 38
- Splitting the Atom 39
- Richie's Revenge 44
- About the Author 46

HOW YOUR YO-YO WORKS

BASICALLY ALL YO-YO'S ARE TWO DISKS JOINED AT THE CENTRE - THE DIFFERENCE COMES WITH HOW YOUR YO-YO IS ATTACHED TO THE STRING.

EARLY YO-YO'S WERE TIED TO THE AXLE, THIS METHOD ALLOWS FOR A SIMPLE UP AND DOWN OR OUT AND BACK MOTION.

IT WAS ONLY AS RECENTLY AS THE LATE 1920'S THAT THE TWISTED LOOP METHOD OF STRINGING A YO-YO WAS INTRODUCED, ALLOWING THE YO-YO TO SPIN AT WHAT APPEARS TO BE THE END OF ITS STRING. EVEN MORE RECENTLY THE USE OF BEARINGS ON THE AXLE (TRANSAXLE) HAVE DRAMATICALLY IMPROVED THE AMOUNT OF SPIN OR SLEEP TIME THAT YOU CAN OBTAIN, OPENING UP THE POSSIBILITIES OF MORE AND MORE COMPLEX TRICKS.

STRING GAP IS ALSO IMPORTANT - MOST YO-YO'S ARE PRESET TO A STANDARD GAP BUT THERE ARE A FEW ON THE MARKET THAT ALLOW FOR STRING GAP ADJUSTMENT - THEY AREN'T CHEAP BUT ARE WORTH CONSIDERATION FOR THE SERIOUS PLAYER.

A SMALLER GAP MAKES FOR EASIER LOOPING, A WIDER GAP IS BETTER FOR SLEEPING AND STRING TRICKS.

AS A MINIMUM YOU SHOULD CHOOSE A LOOPED YO-YO WITH A MAPLE AXLE.

STRING

A YO-YO STRING IS MADE OF COTTON AND IS A TWISTED LOOP. TO ATTACH OR REPLACE THE STRING YOU NEED TO UNTWIST THE END TO FORM A LOOP BIG ENOUGH TO SLIP OVER THE YO-YO.

ON A STANDARD YO-YO ONCE IS ENOUGH - ON A TRANSAXLED YO-YO YOU NEED TO DOUBLE THE LOOP BY TWISTING AND PASSING THE LOOP AROUND A SECOND TIME.

HOW TIGHTLY THE STRING GRABS THE AXLE WILL DICTATE HOW YOUR YO-YO PERFORMS - TIGHTER WILL PRODUCE BETTER LOOPS WHEREAS LOOSER WILL RESULT IN BETTER SLEEP TRICKS

GETTING STARTED

STRING LENGTH
THIS IS DETERMINED BY YOUR HEIGHT. LET THE YO-YO REST ON THE FLOOR WHILE HOLDING THE STRING TRIM TO JUST ABOVE YOUR BELLY BUTTON

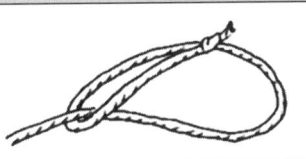

THE SLIPKNOT
MAKE A SLIPKNOT BY TYING THE LOOP IN THE END OF THE STRING AND PASSING THE STRING THROUGH

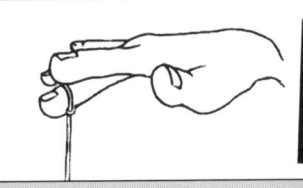

PLACE THE SLIPKNOT OVER THE FIRST KNUCKLE OF YOUR MIDDLE FINGER

WIND UP THE STRING AND WITH PALM UP, PLEASE NOTE THAT THE STRING GOES TO THE TOP OF THE YO-YO, THIS IS IMPORTANT AND IS THE STARTING POSITION FOR ALL THE TRICKS IN THIS BOOK

THAT'S IT! YOU'RE READY TO START!

Splitting the Atom

THE SLEEPER... ...THE SLAPPER

THE SLEEPER
START PALM UP WITH YOUR HAND UP TO YOUR SHOULDER.

THROW THE YO-YO DOWNWARD AND TRY TO ABSORB SOME OF THE ENERGY AS IT APPROACHES THE END OF ITS STRING - IT SHOULD JUST STOP THERE AND SPIN.

SIMPLY **TUG** THE YO-YO TO MAKE IT RETURN TO YOUR HAND. CATCH PALM DOWN. THE **HARDER** YOU THROW, THE **FASTER** IT WILL SPIN.

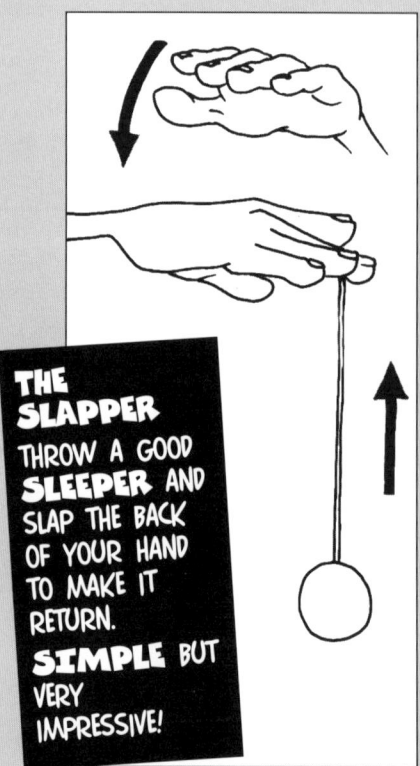

THE SLAPPER
THROW A GOOD **SLEEPER** AND SLAP THE BACK OF YOUR HAND TO MAKE IT RETURN.

SIMPLE BUT VERY IMPRESSIVE!

Splitting the Atom

HOP THE FENCE

HOP THE FENCE
THROW A **SLEEPER***, BUT INSTEAD OF CATCHING IT AS IT COMES BACK...

...GENTLY **FLICK** IT OVER YOUR WRIST AND LET IT GO BACK DOWN, JUST LIKE **LOOP THE LOOP***.

YOU CAN REPEAT THIS OVER AND OVER!

*Sleeper - opposite
*Loop the Loop - page 21

Splitting the Atom

WALK THE DOG...   ...TWO DOGS

WALK THE DOG
FROM A **SLEEPER***, LOWER THE YO-YO TO THE GROUND AND FOLLOW ALONG BEHIND.

AFTER A SHORT STROLL, A SHARP TUG ON THE LEAD WILL BRING THE DOG BACK TO YOUR HAND!

TWO DOGS
TWO YO-YO'S, TWO **SLEEPERS**...
...TWICE AS MUCH FUN?

*Sleeper - page 6

Splitting the Atom

THE CREEPER

THE CREEPER...
AS YOU ARE OUT EXERCISING YOUR DOG ONE DAY, LOWER YOUR HAND TO THE FLOOR...

...A SHARP TUG WILL BRING IT CREEPING BACK TO YOU (MIND YOUR FINGERTIPS!)

Splitting the Atom

JUMP THE DOG

JUMP THE DOG

START **WALKING THE DOG*** FROM BEHIND YOU WITH YOUR HAND ON YOUR HIP TO FORM THE HOOP.

ALLOW IT TO SCAMPER BETWEEN YOUR LEGS...

A SHARP TUG ON THE LEAD WILL BRING THE DOG BACK AND UP THROUGH THE HOOP, OUT IN FRONT OF YOU AND RETURN TO YOUR HAND

*Walk the Dog - page 8

SPAGHETTI

SPAGHETTI

FROM A **SLEEPER***, GATHER UP THE STRING IN SMALL SECTIONS HOLD IN A SPAGHETTI-LIKE BUNCH AND BRING UP TO YOUR MOUTH.

NOW, AS YOU LET GO OF THE STRING, MAKE RIDICULOUS **SLURPING** NOISES AND THE STRING WILL SEEM TO DISAPPEAR INTO YOUR MOUTH!

*Sleeper - page 6

FORWARD PASS

FORWARD PASS

WITH YOUR HAND PALM DOWN, THROW THE YO-YO OUT IN FRONT OF YOU.

AS IT REACHES THE END OF THE STRING IT WILL MOMENTARILY HANG - DEFYING GRAVITY - BEFORE IT RETURNS.

CATCH PALM UP.

AROUND THE WORLD

AROUND THE WORLD

A COMBINATION OF A **FORWARD PASS*** AND A **SLEEPER***.

THROW A GOOD **FORWARD PASS** BUT INSTEAD OF SNAPPING IT BACK, SWING IT AROUND IN A CIRCLE.

HOT TIP - AIM AT 4 O'CLOCK ON THE THROW AND SNAP BACK BETWEEN 3 AND 12 O'CLOCK.

CATCH PALM UP.

(DOES THIS MEAN THAT THE WHOLE WORLD IS IN YOUR HAND?)

*Forward Pass - opposite
*Sleeper - page 6

Splitting the Atom

BREAKAWAY

BREAKAWAY

A variation of the **FORWARD PASS***, thrown across the body and out to one side.

This is the basic throw needed for all of the trapeze tricks

*Forward Pass - page 12

Splitting the Atom

THE DRAWBACK

THE DRAWBACK

WELL, MORE OF AN ADVANTAGE REALLY!

THROW A FAST **SLEEPER**, NOW WITH YOUR FREE HAND GRAB THE STRING BETWEEN YOUR FINGER AND THUMB AND DRAW IT BACK TOWARDS YOU, LIKE A BOW, UNTIL THE YO-YO IS A COUPLE OF INCHES FROM YOUR HAND.

LET GO OF THE STRING AND THE YO-YO WILL SNAP BACK INTO YOUR HAND.

*Sleeper - page 6

THE 3RD DIMENSION

THE 3RD DIMENSION FROM THE **DRAWBACK*** BRING YOUR FREE HAND OUT TO THE SIDE AND SWING THE YO-YO IN A MINIATURE **AROUND THE WORLD*** ARCH.

*The Drawback - page 15
*Around the World - page 13

Splitting the Atom

MONKEY CLIMBS THE STRING & THE ELEVATOR

MONKEY CLIMBS THE STRING

FROM A **SLEEPER**, PLACE THE FOREFINGER OF YOUR FREE HAND ABOUT HALFWAY DOWN THE STRING. BRING YOUR YO-YO HAND DOWN AND FORWARD...

...BRING THE STRING IN FRONT OF THE YO-YO AND, BY GENTLY PULLING YOUR HANDS APART THE LITTLE MONKEY WILL CLIMB. WHEN HE REACHES THE TOP, REMOVE YOUR FINGER FROM THE STRING.

THE ELEVATOR

THIS IS **MONKEY CLIMBS THE STRING** IN REVERSE, BY PULLING THE FREE HAND TOWARDS YOU AND PLACING THE STRING INTO THE BACK GROOVE OF THE YO-YO.

THIS ALLOWS THE YO-YO TO BE MOVED UP AND DOWN THE STRING LIKE A LIFT (SORRY - ELEVATOR)

ROCK THE BABY... OUT WITH THE BATHWATER

ROCK THE BABY

FROM A **SLEEPER**, GRAB THE STRING ABOUT HALFWAY DOWN WITH ALL 4 FINGERS OF YOUR FREE HAND.

NOW BRING THE YO-YO HAND DOWN AND PINCH THE STRING HALFWAY BETWEEN THE FREE HAND AND THE YO-YO, FORMING A TRIANGLE.

NOW BRING THE FREE HAND DOWN UNDER THE YO-YO AND ROCK IT GENTLY.

IT IS A BABY AFTER ALL.

*The 3rd Dimension - page 16

STOP PRESS

OUT WITH THE BATHWATER!

FROM **ROCK THE BABY**, SWING THE BABY UP AROUND AND OUT, AS IN **THE 3RD DIMENSION**.

Splitting the Atom

PINWHEELS... ...SIDEWINDER

PINWHEELS
GRAB THE STRING A FEW INCHES FROM THE YO-YO AND SWING IT THROUGH SMALL **AROUND THE WORLD*** STYLE CIRCLES.

THIS CAN BE DONE FROM ANY OF THE BASIC THROWS AND CAN GO IN EITHER CLOCKWISE OR ANTICLOCKWISE.

SIDEWINDER
THROW HARD AND TO ONE SIDE - THE YO-YO SHOULD SPIN ON ITS SIDE, PARALLEL TO THE FLOOR.

TUG THE YO-YO UP INTO THE AIR, AS IT REACHES THE SAME HEIGHT AS YOUR FREE HAND IT SHOULD RETURN.

*Around the World - page 13

Splitting the Atom

FLYING SAUCER

FLYING SAUCER

THROW A **SIDEWINDER***, PICK UP THE STRING ABOUT 5 OR 6 INCHES FROM THE YO-YO, HOLD FOR A FEW SECONDS, LIFT UPWARDS, AND LET GO.

THE YO-YO WILL RETURN TO BASE!

THIS IS AN EXCELLENT WAY TO TIGHTEN OR LOOSEN THE STRING. DEPENDING ON WHICH WAY YOU THROW

TIP - HELP THINGS ALONG BY FEEDING THE STRING IN WITH THE YO HAND

*Sidewinder - page 19

Splitting the Atom

LOOP THE LOOP

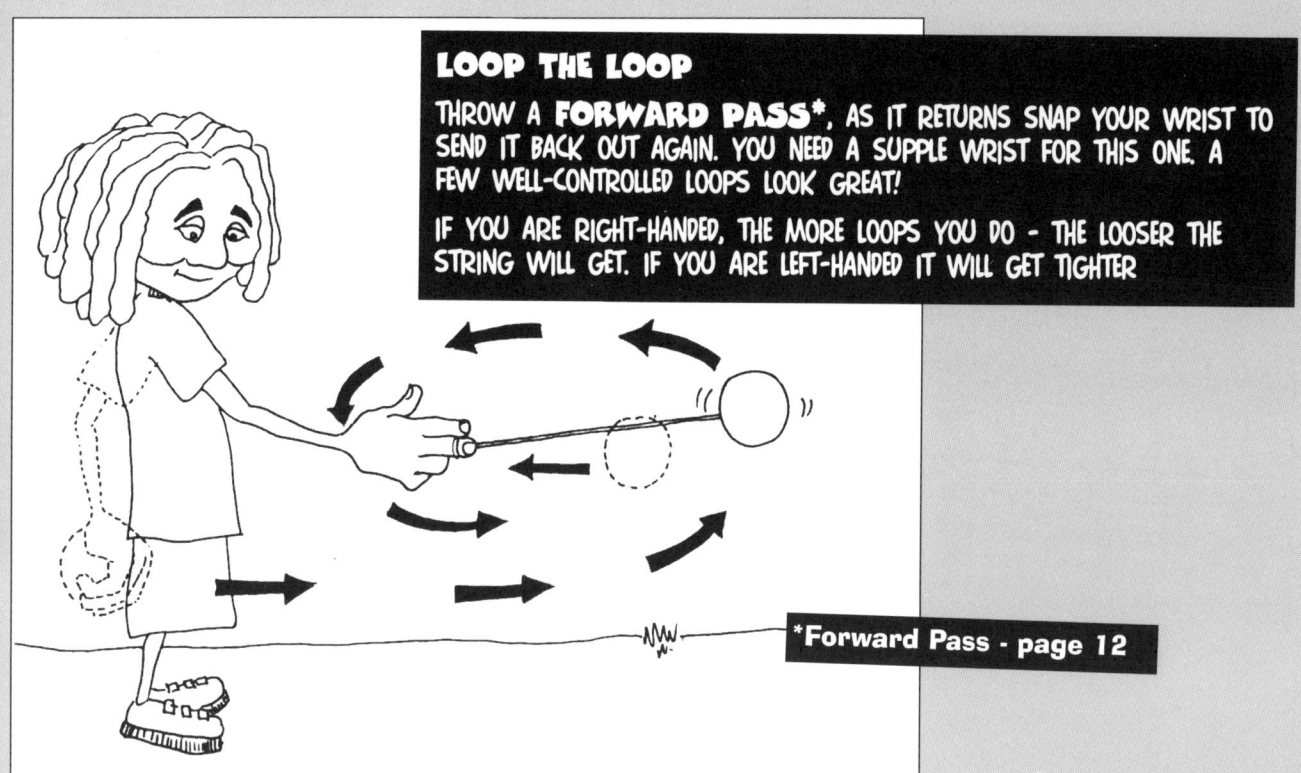

LOOP THE LOOP

THROW A **FORWARD PASS***, AS IT RETURNS SNAP YOUR WRIST TO SEND IT BACK OUT AGAIN. YOU NEED A SUPPLE WRIST FOR THIS ONE. A FEW WELL-CONTROLLED LOOPS LOOK GREAT!

IF YOU ARE RIGHT-HANDED, THE MORE LOOPS YOU DO - THE LOOSER THE STRING WILL GET. IF YOU ARE LEFT-HANDED IT WILL GET TIGHTER

*Forward Pass - page 12

THREE LEAF CLOVER

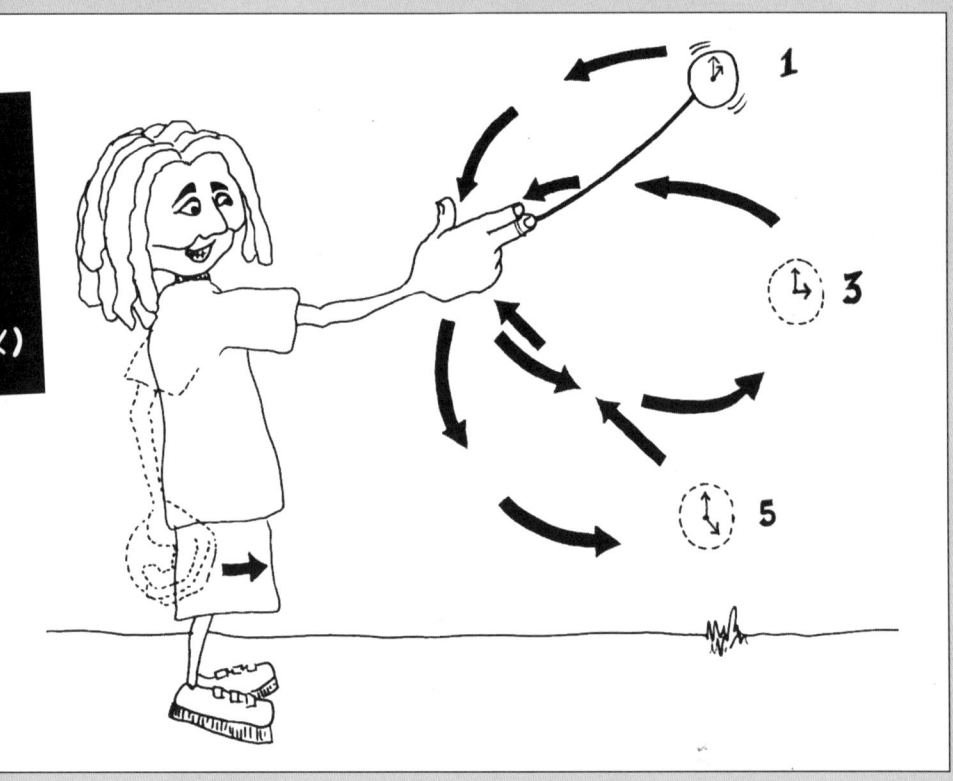

THREE LEAF CLOVER

THROW THE FIRST LOOP UP, THE SECOND LOOP OUT IN FRONT, AND THE THIRD LOOP OUT AND DOWN.

(AIM FOR 1, 3 AND 5 O'CLOCK)

SHOOT FOR THE MOON

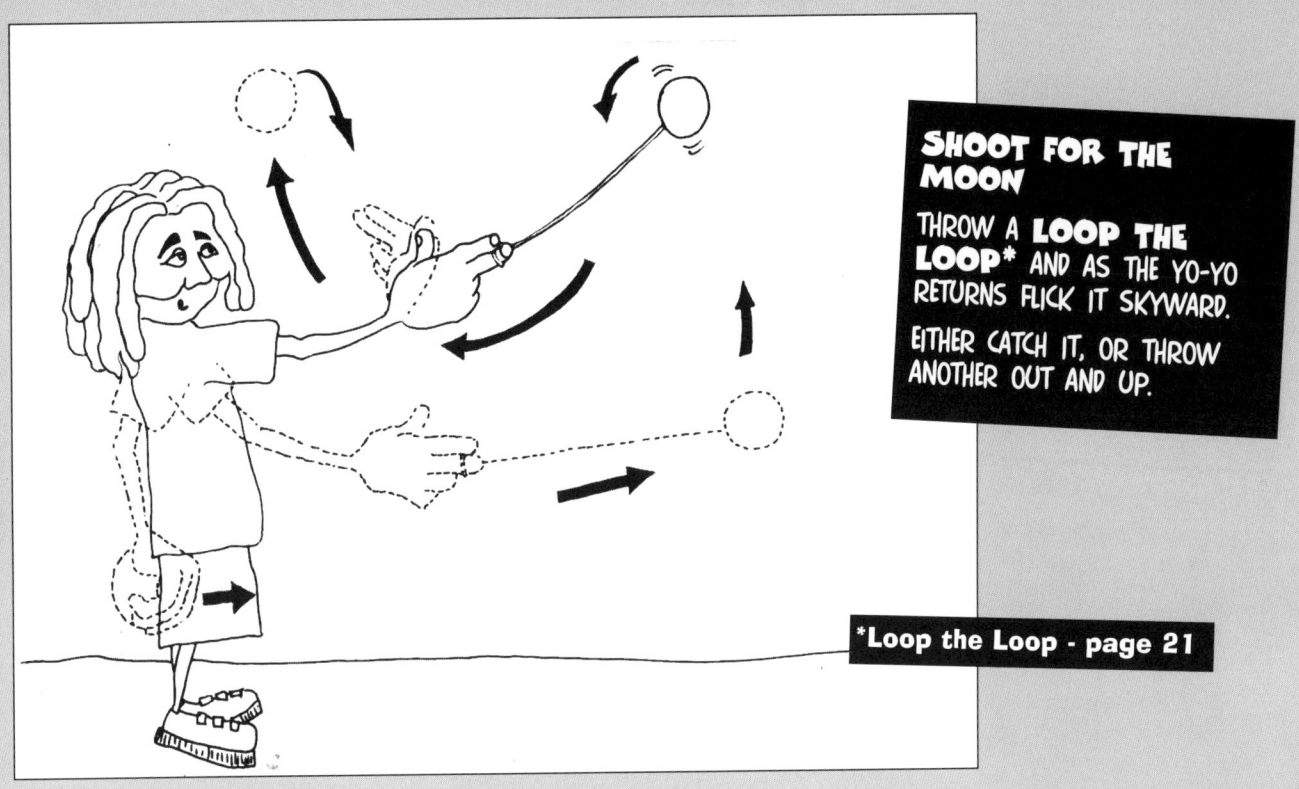

SHOOT FOR THE MOON

THROW A **LOOP THE LOOP*** AND AS THE YO-YO RETURNS FLICK IT SKYWARD.

EITHER CATCH IT, OR THROW ANOTHER OUT AND UP.

*Loop the Loop - page 21

Splitting the Atom

WARP DRIVE

WARP DRIVE

THROW AN **AROUND THE WORLD*** AND THEN, INSTEAD OF CATCHING IT, THROW A **LOOP THE LOOP*** TO BUILD UP SPIN, AND THEN GO **AROUND THE WORLD** AGAIN!

CONTINUE ALTERNATING **AROUND THE WORLD** AND **LOOP THE LOOP** AND SEE HOW MANY YOU CAN DO!

*Around the World - page 13
*Loop the Loop - page 21

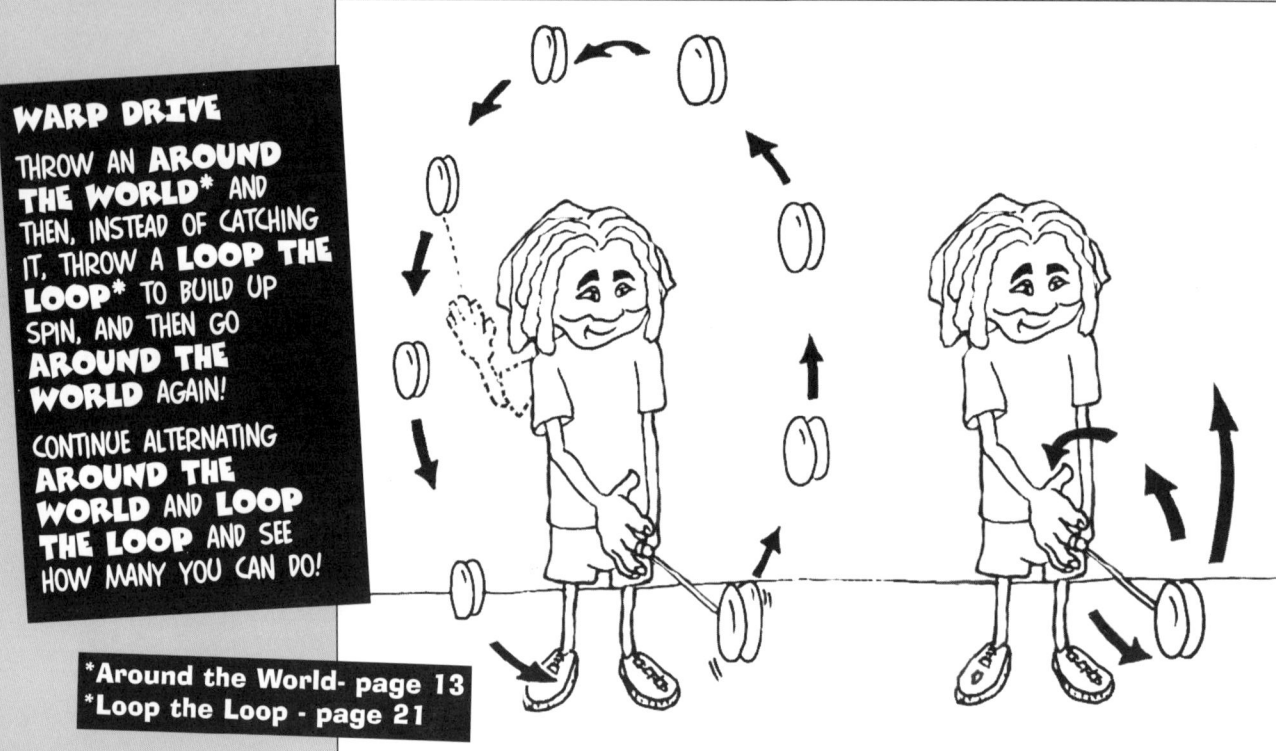

24 Splitting the Atom

THE DRAGSTER

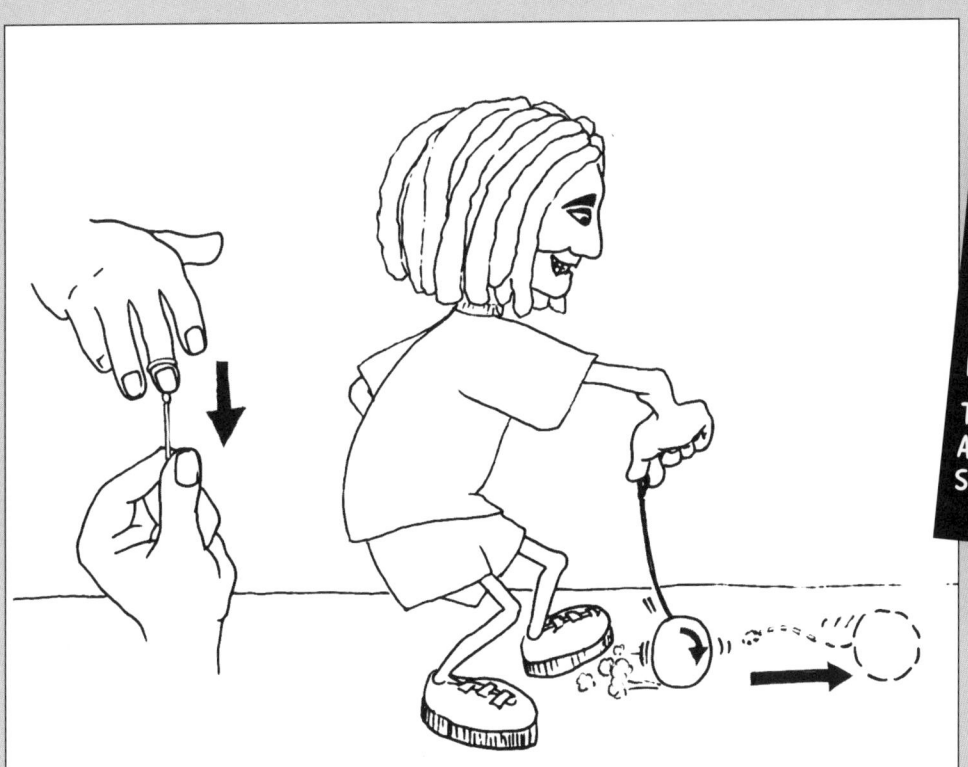

THE DRAGSTER

THROW A **SLEEPER**, THEN REMOVE THE STRING FROM YOUR FINGER AND LOWER THE YO-YO TO THE FLOOR AND LET GO.

THE YO-YO WILL RACE AWAY, DRAGSTER LIKE SOUND EFFECTS AND ALL!

Splitting the Atom

SKY ROCKET

SKY ROCKET

THROW A FAST **SLEEPER** AND UNDO THE STRING FROM YOUR FINGER.

TUG TO MAKE THE YO-YO RETURN AND LET GO OF THE STRING AS IT NEARS YOUR HAND. THE YO-YO WILL CONTINUE SKYWARD - CATCH IT IN YOUR POCKET FOR A COOL FINISH.

Splitting the Atom

SKIN THE CAT

SKIN THE CAT

FROM A **SLEEPER** USE YOUR FREE HAND AS A PULLEY BY BRINGING YOUR YO-YO HAND TOWARDS YOU.

AS TIDDLES APPROACHES YOUR FREE HAND, ENCOURAGE HER UP AND OVER INTO A **FORWARD PASS***.

*Forward Pass - page 12

ORBIT LAUNCH...GUILLOTINE...KICK OVER

ORBIT LAUNCH

FROM A **SLEEPER**, BRING YOUR ELBOW IN FRONT OF THE STRING AND BRING YOUR HAND DOWN.

AT THIS POINT THE YO-YO SHOULD BE HANGING OVER THE BACK OF YOUR ARM...

...TWEAK THE STRING A COUPLE OF INCHES ABOVE THE YO-YO, TO SEND IT UP, OVER AND BACK DOWN IN FRONT OF YOU - AND BACK TO YOUR HAND.

THE GUILLOTINE

..IS THE SAME AS THE **ORBIT LAUNCH** ONLY IT'S AROUND YOUR NECK!

THE KICK OVER

IS AN **ORBIT LAUNCH** BUT INSTEAD OF TWEAKING THE STRING, TAP THE YO-YO UP AND OVER WITH EITHER FOOT.

Splitting the Atom

ROCK THE BABY ON THE LAUNCHPAD

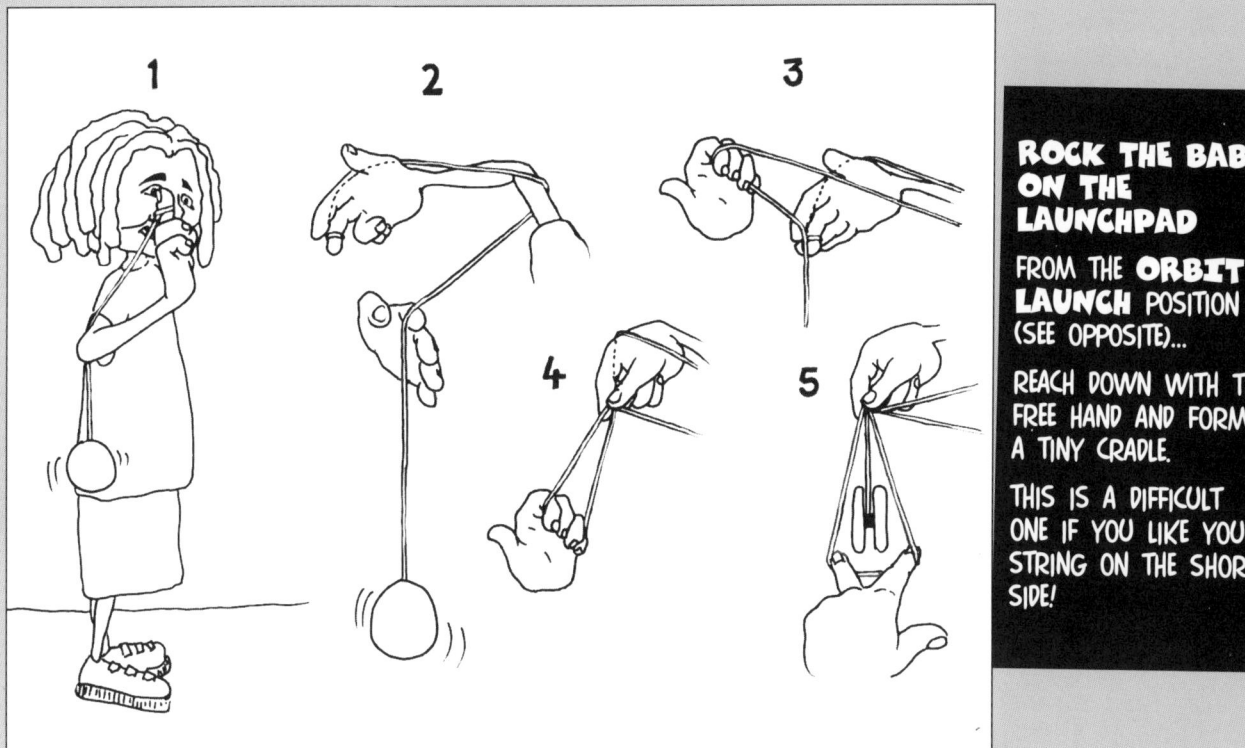

ROCK THE BABY ON THE LAUNCHPAD

FROM THE **ORBIT LAUNCH** POSITION (SEE OPPOSITE)...

REACH DOWN WITH THE FREE HAND AND FORM A TINY CRADLE.

THIS IS A DIFFICULT ONE IF YOU LIKE YOUR STRING ON THE SHORT SIDE!

Splitting the Atom

PULLOVERS

PULLOVERS
USING THE FOREFINGER OF YOUR FREE HAND AS A PULLEY, ENCOURAGE THE YO-YO UP AND OVER AS IT REACHES YOUR FREE HAND.

NOTE FINISHING POSITION, WITH STRING DRAPED OVER YOUR MIDDLE FINGER.

SHOOTING STAR

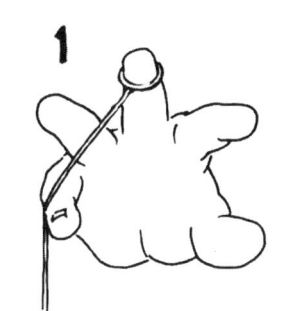
1

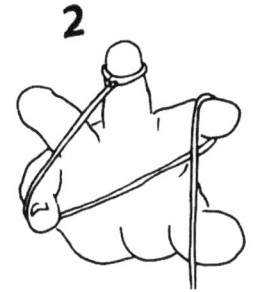
2

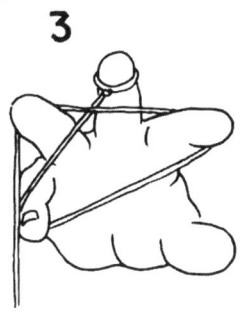
3

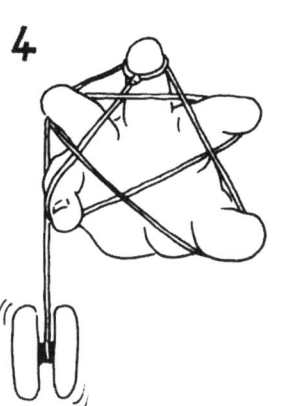
4

SHOOTING STAR

FROM A **SLEEPER** MANOEUVRE THE STRING AROUND YOUR FINGERS IN THIS ORDER:

LITTLE - FORE - RING - THUMB

THEN SWING THE YO-YO OUT IN FRONT OF YOU, ALLOWING THE STRING TO UNRAVEL FROM YOUR FINGERS BEFORE THE YO-YO RETURNS

ROCK THE BABY UNDER THE STARS

FROM A **SHOOTING STAR**, FORM A SMALL CRADLE WITH THE REMAINDER OF THE STRING UNDER THE STAR.

Splitting the Atom

TRAPEZE

TRAPEZE

THROW A **BREAKAWAY***.
INTERCEPT THE STRING WITH THE FOREFINGER OF YOUR FREE HAND A FEW INCHES FROM THE YO-YO, CAUSING IT TO TRAVEL UP AND BACK TOWARDS YOU.

ALLOW THE DARING YOUNG MAN TO LAND GRACEFULLY ON THE STRING.

FINALLY, FLICK HIM SKYWARD TO FINISH.

*Breakaway - page 14

VARIATIONS

BODY SHOTS

INSTEAD OF INTERCEPTING THE STRING WITH YOUR FREE HAND, TRY USING YOUR WRIST, LEG OR NECK.

SINGLE HANDED

THROW A REVERSE **AROUND THE WORLD** SO THAT THE YO-YO TRAVELS UNDER YOUR ARM AND OVER YOUR SHOULDER, LANDING BACK ON THE STRING IN FRONT OF YOU!

Splitting the Atom

ROCK THE BABY ON THE TRAPEZE

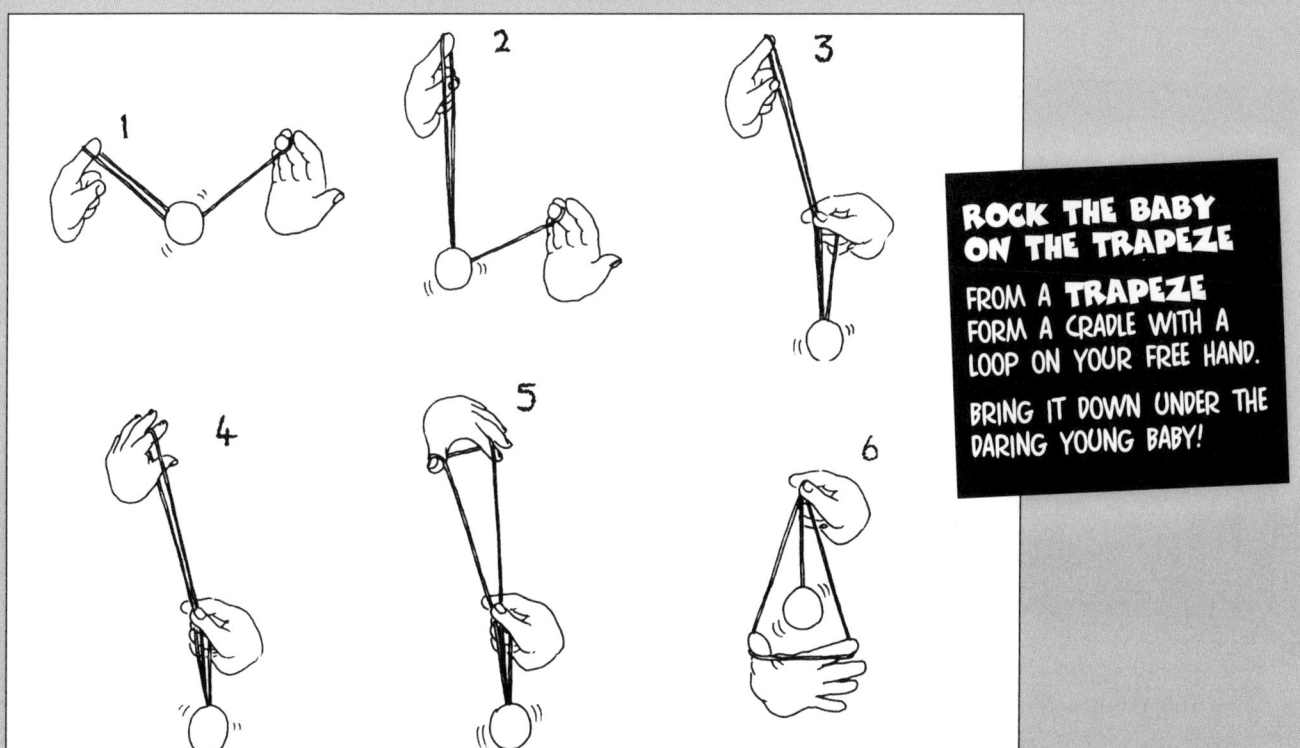

ROCK THE BABY ON THE TRAPEZE

FROM A **TRAPEZE** FORM A CRADLE WITH A LOOP ON YOUR FREE HAND.

BRING IT DOWN UNDER THE DARING YOUNG BABY!

DOUBLE OR NOTHING

DOUBLE OR NOTHING

START AS WITH THE **TRAPEZE*** BUT INSTEAD OF LANDING THE YO-YO ON THE STRING - LET IT CONTINUE ITS FLIGHT AS IN **AROUND THE WORLD*** CATCHING IT ON THE STRING TO FINISH.

*Trapeze - page 32
*Around the World - page 13

Splitting the Atom

DOUBLE SKIN THE CAT

DOUBLE SKIN THE CAT

SKIN THE CAT* TO THE POINT WHERE TIDDLES IS A FEW INCHES FROM YOUR FREE HAND - PASS YOUR FREE HAND AROUND AND UNDER. FROM THIS DOUBLED POSITION TIDDLES WILL BE ABLE TO LOOP TWICE BEFORE FINISHING WITH A **FORWARD PASS*** OR A **LOOP THE LOOP***.

*Skin the Cat - page 27
*Forward Pass - page 12
*Loop the Loop - page 21

STOP AND GO

STOP AND GO

PUSH THE FOREFINGER OF YOUR FREE HAND INTO THE STRING WHILE BRINGING THE YO-YO HAND BACK DOWN AND GUIDING THE STRING INTO THE BACK GROOVE OF THE YO-YO. YOU SHOULD FINISH WITH BOTH HANDS LEVEL, FREE HAND IN FRONT, AND THE YO-YO HANGING FROM THREE STRINGS. TUG UPWARD, SO THE YO-YO WINDS ON ALL THREE STRINGS AND CATCH.

THAT'S THE **STOP** - TO MAKE IT **GO** AGAIN, PULL UPWARDS WITH THE FREE HAND AND THE YO-YO WILL FLY OUT AND BACK TO YOUR HAND. (THIS TRICK IS ALSO KNOWN AS **PERPETUAL MOTION**)

BRAIN TWISTER

THE SECRET OF THIS TRICK IS A WELL FAST **SLEEPER** AND I MEAN **FAST**!

PUSH THE FOREFINGER OF YOUR FREE HAND INTO THE STRING 2/3 OF THE WAY DOWN THE STRING AND PULL THE YO-YO HAND BACK AND ALL THE WAY DOWN, UNDER THE YO-YO. THE STRING FINGER NOW PULLS BACK INTO THE 2 STRINGS SENDING THE YO-YO ON ITS WAY UP AND AWAY.

AS IT UNRAVELS THE YO-YO WILL DESCRIBE A FIGURE 8 IN THE AIR.

Splitting the Atom

FINGER HOP a.k.a. ROLLER COASTER

FINGER HOP

PUSH THE FOREFINGER OF YOUR FREE HAND INTO THE STRING ABOUT 2 INCHES FROM THE YO-YO CAUSING IT TO FLIP UP, OVER YOUR FINGER AND LAND ON THE STRING.

THIS IS A QUICK AND VERY COOL WAY OF GETTING INTO THE CORRECT POSITION FOR THE LAST THREE TRICKS

*Trapeze - page 32

BARREL ROLLS

FROM A **FINGER HOP**, PLACE YOUR YO-YO FINGER INTO THE LOOP JUST BELOW THE FOREFINGER OF YOUR FREE HAND. PUSH FORWARD AND BRING DOWN UNDER AND AROUND THE YO-YO. NOW REPEAT THIS ACTION USING THE FOREFINGER OF YOUR FREE HAND.

WITH A LITTLE PRACTICE YOU CAN MOVE BOTH HANDS AROUND THE YO-YO IN A CONTINUOUS PEDALLING MOTION.

(THIS CAN ALSO BE DONE FROM A **TRAPEZE***)

Splitting the Atom

SPLITTING THE ATOM

THIS IS A VERY COMPLEX TRICK AND IS REALLY A COMBINATION OF MANY MOVES ALREADY DESCRIBED IN THIS BOOK. **DON'T** EXPECT TO LEARN THIS IN A DAY - TAKE IT STEP BY STEP AND YOU WILL GET THERE.

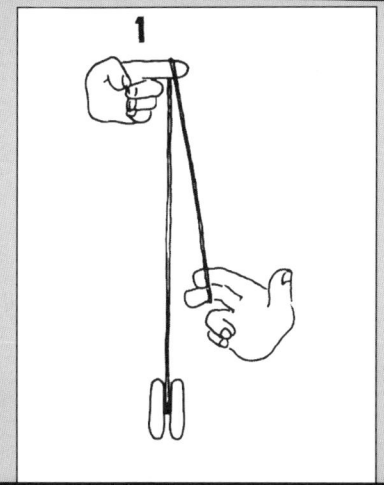

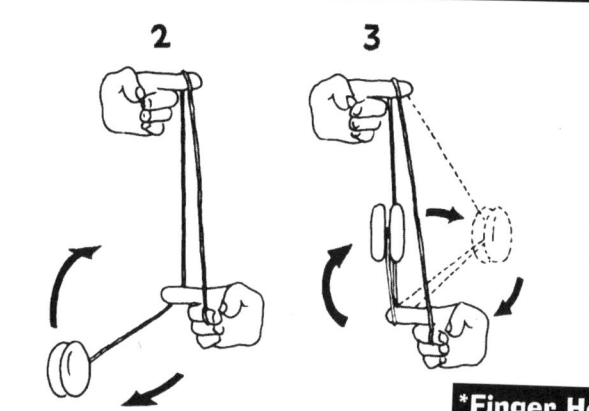

START WITH A FAST **SLEEPER** AND DRAPE THE STRING OVER THE FOREFINGER OF YOUR FREE HAND

PUSH THE FOREFINGER OF YOUR YO-YO HAND INTO THE STRING AS IN THE **FINGER HOP***, CATCHING THE YO-YO ON THE FAR STRING.

*Finger Hop - opposite

MORE OVER THE PAGE...

SPLITTING THE ATOM (continued)...

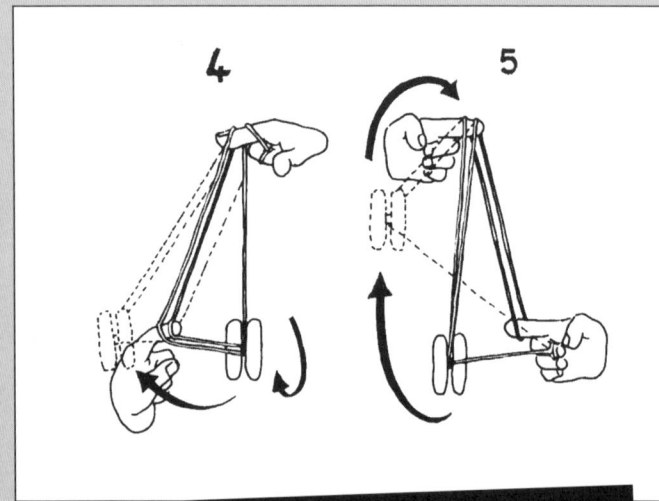

PULL UP AND TOWARDS YOU ON THE DOUBLE STRINGS, CAUSING THE WHOLE ARRANGEMENT TO SWING UP AND OVER THE YO-YO HAND.

THIS ACTION CAN BE REPEATED AS OFTEN AS YOU DARE. PROBABLY BEST TO DO JUST THE ONE WHILE LEARNING!

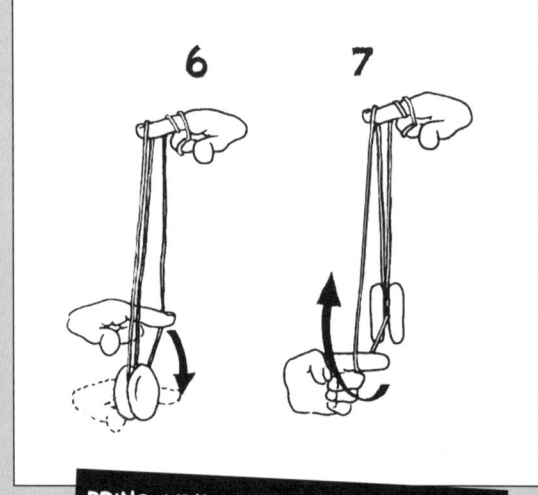

BRING YOUR FREE HAND FORWARD, DOWN AND UNDER THE YO-YO AND BACK UP TO ABOUT HALFWAY UP THE BUNCH OF STRINGS

...SPLITTING THE ATOM...

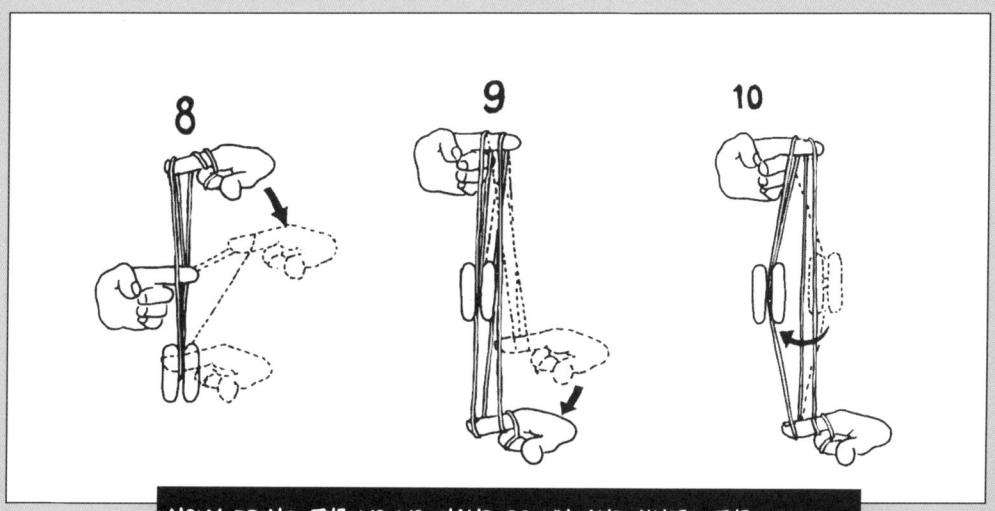

NOW BRING THE YO-YO HAND DOWN AND UNDER THE YO-YO TO CATCH THE STRING IN THE GROOVE AS IT PASSES UNDER.

IT'S NOT OVER YET! MORE OVER THE PAGE!

SPLITTING THE ATOM (continued)...

YOU SHOULD NOW HAVE THE YO-YO SUSPENDED BY TWO LOOPS FROM YOUR FREE HAND.

DROP THE LOOP NEAREST THE END OF YOUR FINGER AND YOU SHOULD BE IN THE CORRECT POSITION TO EXECUTE THE **BRAIN TWISTER***

SO **DO** THE **BRAIN TWISTER***! (ALMOST THERE)

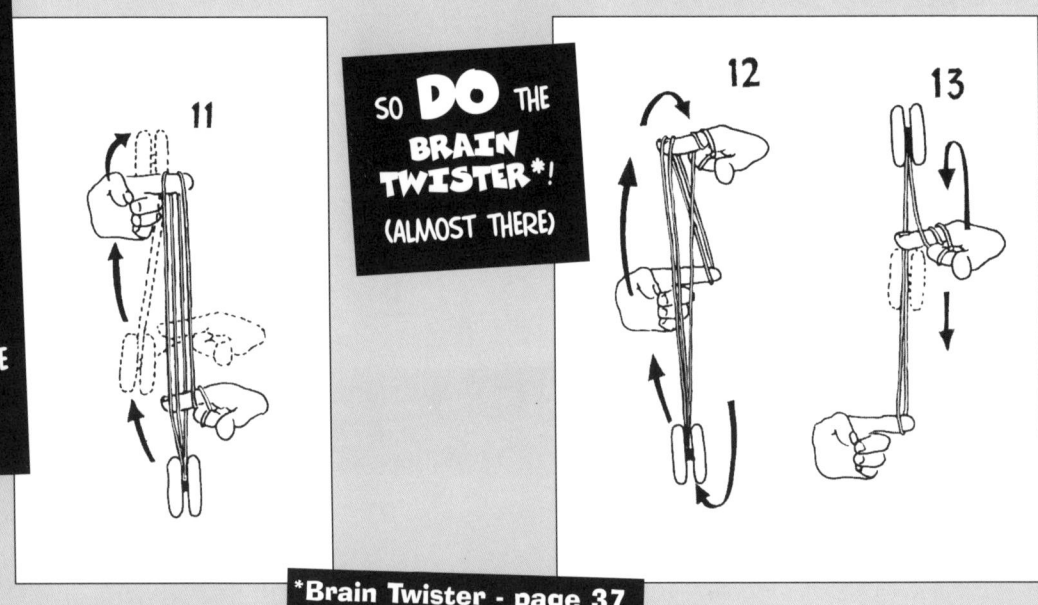

*Brain Twister - page 37

42 Splitting the Atom

...SPLITTING THE ATOM

...FINISH WITH A **DOUBLE SKIN THE CAT*** AND MAYBE A FEW **LOOP THE LOOPS*** OR **WARP DRIVES*** INTO A **TRAPEZE*** AND....

*Double Skin the Cat - page 35
*Loop the Loop - page 21
*Warp Drive - page 24
*Trapeze - page 32

WELCOME TO ADVANCED YO-YOING!!!

RICHIE'S REVENGE

HERE'S AN EXAMPLE OF A COMBINATION OF TRICKS...

PRACTICE EACH TRICK AND THEN STRING THEM TOGETHER IN THE FOLLOWING ORDER

(EACH ONE SHOULD LEAD SMOOTHLY TO THE NEXT)

1. SLEEPER (PAGE 6)

2. PULLOVER (PAGE 30)

3. FINGER HOP (PAGE 38)

4. BRAIN TWISTER (PAGE 37)

RICHIE'S REVENGE

PINWHEEL (PAGE 19)

LOOP THE LOOP (PAGE 21)

AROUND THE WORLD (PAGE 13)

TRAPEZE (PAGE 32)

THAT'S ONE FULL CYCLE

NOW IF YOU TURN YOUR BODY 180 DEGREES AND SLIGHTLY REARRANGE THE FREE HAND FINGER IN THE LOOP YOU ARE BACK TO STAGE 4, SO IN THEORY YOU COULD CONTINUE THE SEQUENCE INDEFINITELY!

THE KEY TO THE TRICK IS IN STAGES 6 AND 7 - ALSO KNOWN AS THE **WARP DRIVE** - AS THIS **REVERSES** THE SPIN ON THE YO-YO AND **SPEEDS** IT UP AGAIN.

Splitting the Atom

ABOUT THE AUTHOR

Richie Windsor (no relation) is 34, he learnt to juggle at the age of 18. By the age of 20, he had given up his job as a painter and decorator and was earning his living as a professional juggler, working all over the world.

In the past 14 years he has visited most of Europe, working on street, screen and stage. Some of the more memorable include a hydraulic stage in Malta, and a theatre in Sarajévo, Bosnia, during the war.

He takes a broad view of juggling and sees it as object manipulation and is still amazed at what can be achieved through repetitive practice and sheer determination in search of perfection.

Richie became interested in the yo-yo three years ago when he took over a small market stall, selling juggling equipment. That developed into "Airtime" - Exeter based specialists in objects that require human interaction and endeavour such as - juggling equipment, kites, boomerangs and yo-yos.

Some of the most important things in his life at the moment are, his computer, yo-yos, quadline kites, shopfittings and music.

Finally, the five most important people in his life are his wonderfully tolerant and lovely wife, Jackie, and their fantastically naughty boys - Josh, Isaac, Jake and Louis